Original title:
Life, Laughs, and Little Answers

Copyright © 2025 Creative Arts Management OÜ
All rights reserved.

Author: Jaxon Kingsley
ISBN HARDBACK: 978-1-80566-239-6
ISBN PAPERBACK: 978-1-80566-534-2

Sprinkles of Cheer

A jellybean dance in a crowded room,
Giggles explode like a colorful boom.
Under the table, a shoe goes astray,
It's just another twist in a silly ballet.

With muffins that giggle and cupcakes that sing,
Who knew dessert could be such a fling?
Each bite a chuckle, a burst of delight,
Sprinkles on top make the day feel just right.

The Art of Being Present

Staring at clouds, they take funny shapes,
A dragon, a duck, and three silly apes.
What if they talk, in a whimsical game,
Where dreams mix with laughter and nothing's the same?

Balloons float away with a giggle and cheer,
Chasing them down feels like a wild deer.
In the midst of our antics, time slips like sand,
We dance in the moment, no plans are at hand.

Mirth in Motion

Running down streets with our hair in a whirl,
Dodging small puddles, we give them a twirl.
A slide on some grass, we tumble with grace,
Giggling echoes, we leave our trace.

With friends by our side, there's mischief to find,
Jokes whispered softly, the kind that's unkind.
Each moment we share, a treasure we hoard,
In the book of our days, it's laughter we stored.

Whispered Secrets of the Heart

A kitten who sneezes, oh what a delight,
Trips on its paws, lands in a pile of light.
Each whisker a story, each purr a sweet song,
It makes us a family, where giggles belong.

Secrets we cherish hidden away,
Like socks that get lost in the dryer each day.
But laughter, we find, is the best kind of art,
Painting our moments, whispered from the heart.

Small Treasures in the Vastness of Now

Tiny sparks of joy we find,
In the crumbs of daily grind.
A sock that vanished, now it's back,
A giggle hides in winter's crack.

In a teacup, dreams unfold,
Songs are sung, yet never told.
A dance with shadows on the wall,
Even silence can have a ball.

Moments passed, like quickening light,
Chasing shadows through the night.
A squirrel's leap, a child's gaze,
Small treasures fill mundane days.

So raise a glass, let spirits soar,
To small delights we can't ignore.
For in the chaos, laughter grows,
Through twist and turns, the fun just flows.

Curious Tales from the Heart's Archive

Once a cat wore shoes too tight,
Strolled around, such a silly sight.
With every step, a comical dance,
Turning heads, sparking chance.

Old letters filled with love and woe,
Revealed the truth, then stole the show.
A lovebird's nefarious schemes,
Crafting plots in quirky dreams.

Grandpa's tales of wizards bold,
Of frogs that croaked, and secrets told.
Each laugh a treasure, pure and bright,
In the warmly woven night.

Serendipity sings in the air,
As we gather stories, show we care.
For in each tale, a giggle waits,
Curious moments that love creates.

Moments in the Sun

Sunny days bring laughter loud,
Children chase, a merry crowd.
Sandcastles rise with dreams so grand,
Fingers sticky from ice cream hand.

The old dog snores in warm embrace,
While treetops sway with careful grace.
A sudden splash, a joyful shout,
In the sun, there's no room for doubt.

Picnic spread on the grass so green,
With cheeky ants, a daring scene.
Every snack is a feast of cheer,
To heartily laugh, that's why we're here.

As sunsets glow and shadows fade,
We hold these moments, unafraid.
For in the warmth of shared delight,
The mundane dances, thriving bright.

Whispers of Joy

In the morning, a coffee cheer,
Stirring dreams while skies are clear.
A bird outside sings sweet refrain,
Reminding us to dance in rain.

With simple things, we find our glee,
A joke exchanged, a cup of tea.
Beneath the stars, the stories play,
Whispers of joy lead the way.

Tiny feet and laughter burst,
In everyday moments, we trust.
A tickle fight, a pillow fort,
In these small battles, hearts cavort.

So lift your voice, let spirits ring,
For in the silly, we discover spring.
Through whispers shared, life shines so bright,
In the laughter, we find our light.

The Ripple of Smiles

A giggle bounced upon the breeze,
Like squirrels chatting in the trees.
A wink exchanged, a joke retold,
Turns moments into glimmers bold.

The sun dips low, the shadows play,
As children frolic, shout, and sway.
With silly faces, fun unfolds,
As laughter's warmth, like sunlight, holds.

The ice cream drips down on the cone,
A tasty mess, yet not alone.
We share the sprinkles, joy combined,
In every giggle, bliss we find.

So let the chatter twirl and whirl,
In every laugh, our hearts unfurl.
For in this world of silly schemes,
Laughter reigns and brightly beams.

Weaving Whispers

Whispers of joy in a crowded room,
A slice of cake, a lilac bloom.
A joke on lips, bright eyes that twinkle,
Sharing a moment, hearts that crinkle.

In shadows cast by flickering light,
Laughter dances, taking flight.
With every snort and hearty cheer,
We weave the fabric of good cheer.

A kitten's pounce, a puppy's bark,
Each tiny mishap leaves a mark.
As giggles echo through the night,
We savor mischief wrapped in delight.

So gather 'round, bring your best smile,
Stay a little longer, let's chat awhile.
For in these whispers, warm and free,
We find the magic, just you and me.

Tides of Joy

Waves of chuckles crest and break,
On shores of fun where we awake.
Seagulls squawk in perfect tune,
Making mischief beneath the moon.

A sandcastle crowned in wobbly might,
With seashells shining, what a sight!
The ocean's giggle, a gentle tease,
As sunbeams ripple through the breeze.

Turn up the music, dance along,
With friends beside, we sing our song.
From twirls to jitters, we won't sit still,
In every heartbeat, joy we feel.

So ride the surge, let worries drift,
As summer's glow becomes our gift.
In this ocean, wild and bright,
Laughter shines like stars at night.

Mirthful Musings

In quiet corners, thoughts take flight,
With playful dreams that feel so right.
A whimsical thought, a playful twist,
In every moment, joy can't be missed.

As clouds roll by in shapes of cheer,
We chase the sun, we conquer fear.
A slip, a trip, a pie on the face,
Transforms a frown into a smile's grace.

Through silly stories, wisdom grows,
In every chuckle, warmth overflows.
So gather 'round for tales anew,
Where laughter lingers, bright and true.

For life's a canvas, colors blend,
With strokes of joy, we make amends.
In mirthful musings, we shall find,
A secret laughter, intertwined.

Sweet Whimsy of the Wandering Soul

With a skip and a hop, they roam so wide,
Chasing shadows and giggles, with hearts open wide.
A pizza slice talks, as do rubber bands,
In this playful realm, all nonsense stands.

The hats on the sidewalk have secrets to share,
While the clouds do a jig, floating up in the air.
Socks flirt with slippers while shoes try to dance,
Every tiny moment, just a merry chance.

Puzzles Wrapped in the Ordinary

A spoon's quest for soup, a hunter's delight,
While forks hold a meeting, discussing their plight.
The blender sings sweetly, a tune all its own,
Spinning dreams of milkshakes in every home.

Chairs whisper secrets in the corner of rooms,
As pillows plot schemes under silken moon blooms.
Cups gather stories, each one a unique,
In the warmth of the kitchen, where laughter can peek.

Joyful Nudges from the Universe

Stars wink conspiratorially, just after dusk,
While crickets compose symphonies, full of musk.
A breeze brings a chuckle from trees standing tall,
As the moon plays magician, captivating all.

Raindrops giggle as they tumble and spin,
Creating puddles where reflections begin.
In this cosmic theater, the antics are grand,
With each passing moment, a nudge from the hand.

The Canvas of Quirky Encounters

A penguin in sandals walks down to the sea,
While a cactus in sunglasses declares, 'Look at me!'
Their stories entwine in a waltz with the tide,
As laughter spills over, and time takes a ride.

The clouds toss confetti, while rainbows take flights,
Chasing butterflies painted in dappled lights.
In this odd little dreamscape, all fun is profound,
With each little moment, joyfully unbound.

Puzzles of the Soul

In the game of thought, I try to play,
Finding meaning in the words I say.
Each riddle twists, a curious dance,
Who knew wisdom could wear such pants?

Fingers crossed while I pause to think,
A cup of coffee, then a blink.
Cracking codes like a nutty squirrel,
Wishing for answers that make me whirl.

Life's a puzzle, each piece misplaced,
I'm just a jester in a comical chase.
With questions floating like balloons in the air,
Chasing laughs like shadows, unaware.

So I shuffle along with a chuckle loud,
Dancing on answers, feeling so proud.
In riddles and giggles, I find my way,
In this jigsaw of joy, I'll forever stay.

Sprouts of Hope

Tiny seeds in the garden of cheer,
Sprouting stories that tickle the ear.
With sunbeams dancing upon my head,
I plant my dreams, and then I'm fed.

Little sprouts with big ideas bloom,
Waving their leaves, making room.
Each giggle a petal, each sigh a stem,
Creating a garden no one can condemn.

When clouds roll in, and shadows play,
I find my way to the sunny bay.
With laughter as water, I take my chance,
And watch those sprouts do a goofy dance.

In this patch of sunshine, all colors blend,
With hopes growing wild around every bend.
So here's to the sprouts, both small and bright,
In their cheerful garden, it feels so right.

Melodies of the Everyday

Chirping birds sing a silly song,
As I stumble through, trying to belong.
With mismatched socks and hair askew,
Every minute a verse, it's all brand new.

The kettle whistles like a cheeky friend,
And the clock ticks on, refusing to bend.
With each clink of spoon, a rhythmic beat,
In this symphony of chaos, life's a treat.

Stumbling on beats, I dance with grace,
In the grocery line, I find my place.
With laughter ringing like bells in the night,
Every little moment feels so right.

So let's whistle along, through thick and thin,
Finding joy in the mess, where we begin.
In this melody sweet, I'll take my stand,
We're all just notes in a playful band.

Short and Sweet Discoveries

On a rooftop tall, I found a joke,
It danced around like a jubilant smoke.
With punchlines hiding beneath the sun,
I jotted them down, we're never done.

A cookie crumb falls as I snack and wink,
A tiny treasure that makes me think.
In the search for humor, I inquired,
Each laugh a spark, I felt inspired.

From puddles reflecting those silly skies,
To giggles caught in the wind's soft sighs.
Every corner hides a playful twist,
In discoveries short, we find our bliss.

So here's a toast to those joyous finds,
In the ordinary, we unearth the binds.
With light hearts embracing each grin with glee,
Every moment a chance, wild and free.

A Tapestry of Smiles in Time's Flow

In the garden of jesting blooms,
Where whimsy dances with the brooms,
Giggles hang like fruit on trees,
As time flows gently, like a breeze.

Chasing shadows, we find delight,
In silly tales under moonlight,
With each chuckle, bonds are made,
In this merry masquerade.

Juggling troubles, we spin around,
Finding humor where hope abounds,
In laughter's echo, troubles fade,
A patchwork quilt, cheerfully laid.

As wrinkles form from grinning wide,
We cherish moments side by side,
In every giggle, joy is sewn,
A tapestry of love we've grown.

Hummingbirds and Hiccups of Fate

The smallest things can make us smile,
Like hummingbirds that flit a while,
In the garden of odd delight,
Where hiccups turn to purest light.

With hiccups that echo through the air,
We laugh at moments unaware,
Fate's quirks dance upon our skin,
In the rhythm of a cheerful spin.

Chasing laughter like a fleeting star,
Finding joy in your own bizarre,
As fate trips lightly, don't despair,
For whimsy floats upon the air.

In this game of twists and turns,
We collect the giggles and the burns,
For in the end, amidst the strife,
We find the beauty in our life.

Idioms of Innocence and Imagination

In worlds where dreams and fancies play,
Innocence blooms in a glorious sway,
With every idiom spun from light,
We weave our tales, oh what a sight!

Imagination runs wild and free,
Crafting stories as sweet as can be,
With giggles tucked behind our ears,
We chase the shadows, lose our fears.

Each phrase a puzzle, colorful design,
In moments bright, our hearts align,
Like children lost in a carnival dream,
Finding joy in the silliest scheme.

As the sun sets, we twirl and sway,
In innocence, we find our way,
Through laughter's lens, we clearly see,
The magic in simplicity.

Grins and Grains of Sand

On sun-kissed shores where breezes sway,
Grains of sand whisper tales of play,
With each footprint, laughter lifts the tide,
We cherish each moment, side by side.

In the bright sun, shadows shimmy and tease,
As grins emerge like gentle sea breeze,
Each splash a serenade, joyful and sweet,
In the dance of waves, our hearts find their beat.

With buckets and spades, we craft our dreams,
In playful patterns, life brightly beams,
Through the laughter, the world feels grand,
As we gather joy like grains of sand.

Even as tides attempt to erase,
The memories we carve, the smiles we chase,
In the wink of a wave, we'll always find,
The treasures we keep are joyfully designed.

Brewing Happiness

In the kitchen, pots collide,
Spilling dreams on the side.
A pinch of giggles, a dash of cheer,
Stirring up fun as we draw near.

Cookies dance on the counter, bright,
Syrup drizzles—a sugary sight.
With each whisk, a chuckle shared,
In this chaos, joy is bared.

Laughter bubbles, warm and free,
Like a teapot, we bask in glee.
Sprinkling smiles, a recipe true,
Cooking up memories, just me and you.

The Echo of Innocent Joy

A child's giggle flutters like wings,
Chasing shadows that winter brings.
Skipping stones on a pond so wide,
Ripples of laughter, a joyful ride.

Through sunlit fields, we run and play,
Gathering moments; they never stray.
Slipping on grass, oh what a show,
Rolling in daisies, stealing the glow.

Innocence wrapped in melodies sweet,
Chirping crickets join our upbeat.
Echoes of joy in the soft twilight,
Whispering secrets that feel just right.

Joyrides Through Ordinary

Two spoons in one big bowl,
Flickering candles, feeling whole.
A ride on bikes through streets so loud,
Each bump and giggle makes us proud.

Park benches where stories collide,
Old and young take a whimsical ride.
From playful swings to slides that squeak,
Every moment's magic, spontaneous and unique.

Sunshine dripping through maple trees,
Lemonade stands and summer breeze.
We'll paint the town in colors bright,
Finding glee in the everyday light.

Hues of Heartstrings

A splash of color on a canvas rare,
With each brushstroke, we catch despair.
Blues and yellows mix and spin,
Transforming frowns into goofy grins.

Puppies barking, laughter's flare,
Twisting dreams float in the air.
Rainbow socks and mismatched shoes,
Dancing like we've got nothing to lose.

In the gallery of our hearts displayed,
Each hue a moment, never to fade.
Embracing quirks with every beat,
In this art, we find our sweet.

Unraveled Mysteries

In the depths of a puzzling night,
Questions dance in the pale moonlight.
A sock runs off, where can it be?
Lost in the dryer, sipping sweet tea.

The cat wears a hat, thinks he's a king,
Chasing shadows, what joy they bring.
Why do we trip over things left behind?
A riddle that's sweeter than any refined.

Cupcakes giggle with frosting so bright,
Yet, why do they vanish by morning light?
Sneaky little munchkins, they're up to no good,
Like sneezes that dance in the heart of the wood.

Wobbly chairs and a creaky floor,
Join the fun, let your worries out the door.
A toast to the quirks that make us cheer,
For odd little moments we hold so dear.

Sunlit Journeys

Took a stroll down the winding way,
Sunshine whispers, 'Come out and play!'
In puddles of laughter, we splashed all around,
Each giggle a treasure waiting to be found.

Pigeons parade in their feathery suits,
Chasing crumbs, oh how they hoot!
A playful breeze musses my hair,
How can this day be anything but fair?

Bicycles wobble, riders hold tight,
Squealing with joy as we take flight.
One shoe's missing, oh what a sight,
But we roll on, hearts soaring so bright.

With splattered paint and mismatched socks,
Each moment's a fortune in quirky paradox.
So let's dance with the daffodils by the way,
For today's little whims won't ever decay.

Fragments of Cheer

A sprinkle of giggles and a dash of fun,
Tiny moments where we all can run.
Lemonade dreams in a paper cup,
With silly straws, we drink them up.

Who stole the cookies? Oh, what a crime!
The culprit is sneaky, always on time.
With crumbs on their face and a glittery grin,
We just can't help but let the chuckles begin.

Juggling socks and mismatched shoes,
Every stumble becomes good news.
Puns floating like bubbles in the air,
Catch one and giggle, if you dare.

The clock ticks in polka-dot attire,
It dances and twirls, taking us higher.
So let's embrace every bumble and jest,
In a world of fragments, we truly are blessed.

Curious Contrasts

Under the stars, a frog plays a tune,
While a cat in a bow tie dances by moon.
Butterflies ponder in elegant style,
As ants do the cha-cha, each step full of guile.

Marshmallows float on a river of cream,
While pickles play chess and plot for a dream.
Who knew the world could be upside down?
With giggles and grins, we turn it around.

Rain falls in colors, a cotton candy splash,
As umbrellas spin in a whimsical clash.
We chase after raindrops, believing the tale,
That laughter and wonders will always prevail.

So let's spin in circles, ignite our fun,
In a curious contrast, we all become one.
With a wink and a nudge, let's frolic for cheers,
In a carnival world that dissolves all our fears.

Chasing Rainbows on Pebbled Paths

Beneath the sky, colors swirl and sway,
Pebbles giggle, dance, come what may.
With every step, a chuckle unfolds,
As silly secrets the brightness holds.

Hopping past puddles, we splash and skitter,
Each droplet sparkles, a glint and a glitter.
We chase the hues through laughter and cheer,
Finding joy where the path is unclear.

The sun paints smiles on each bouncing face,
While breezes tickle in warm embrace.
Dancing in circles, spinning around,
In our playful world, glee knows no bounds.

So gather your dreams, let's chase the light,
Through pebbled paths, laughter takes flight.
For in every step, a joke will arise,
As rainbows dance in our playful skies.

Inquisitive Hues on the Palette of Day

With brushes in hand, we paint our delight,
As questions bloom, vibrant and bright.
What color is giggle, or joy in a jar?
Mixed with the sun, it shines like a star.

The canvas whispers, 'Let's splash and explore,'
Each stroke a chuckle, begging for more.
In the shades of bliss, curiosity beams,
As each little question ignites all our dreams.

We dip and we dive into oceans of hue,
Mix blues with the pinks, create something new.
And as the laughter colors the air,
We find little answers hidden with care.

So let's paint the world with silly delight,
Inquisitive hues that tickle the night.
With laughter our palette, let's splash and sway,
Creating a masterpiece every day!

Chuckles in the Symphony of Being

In the symphony of sounds, giggles take flight,
Notes twirl in the air, a playful sight.
Each chuckle and snort, a rhythm anew,
Composing the melody of me and you.

The trumpets of joy, with a blaring grin,
While laughter's soft strings draw us all in.
Drumming on tables, tapping our toes,
In this crazy orchestra, humor just flows.

The violins sing of mischief and cheer,
In the cacophony, there's nothing to fear.
With every punchline, the audience roars,
In this silly concert, we open new doors.

So come dance around, let your spirit be free,
In this joyful tune, you're invited to be.
Chuckles resound in this playful spree,
Where the symphony of being is wild and carefree.

Whimsical Footprints Across the Cosmos

Starry nights call with a humorous tune,
As we leave goofy prints on the silver moon.
Each step a giggle, each laugh a twirl,
In this cosmic dance, dreams unfurl.

We bounce on stardust, glide on a whim,
With planets as playgrounds, we swing and swim.
Tickled by comets, we ride their trails,
In this whimsical journey, laughter prevails.

Shooting stars grin as they zoom far and wide,
While aliens wiggle, join in for the ride.
With quirky companions, the universe sings,
In our celestial waltz, we adorn crowns of wings.

So let's gather smiles from the lamps in the sky,
And share them with galaxies zipping by.
For in each silly step as we roam the vast sea,
We find little treasures of joy, wild and free.

Unraveling Threads of the Everyday

In a world of tangled yarns,
The sock parade takes flight,
With one missing, one it mourns,
What a strange delight!

A coffee cup, half full, half shy,
Jumps from the desk with glee,
'You can't catch me!' it seems to cry,
Oh, the joy we see!

When toast lands butter-side down,
Laughter echoes, a silly sound,
As crumbs dance all around,
In chaos, joy is found.

With every spill and every fall,
We find a tale to tell,
In the most mundane, we stand tall,
Finding odd magic that fits so well.

Sunbeams and Silly Questions

Chasing rays that laugh and play,
A cat in a sunbeam sprawls,
Does it think and drift away,
While answering cosmic calls?

Why does the sandwich play hide and seek,
In the back of the fridge so cold?
It whispers secrets, soft and meek,
Of adventures yet untold.

Rain boots dance in puddles wide,
With splashes that chase the frowns,
In every droplet, joy will bide,
While the world keeps turning 'round.

Bright colors splash across the day,
What's next on the to-do list?
With silly whims, we sing and sway,
In laughter, we find our twist.

Moments that Make the Heart Skip

When the clock strikes an odd time,
And the cat does a silly prance,
We find ourselves lost in rhyme,
Life's a comical dance.

A hat worn sideways with flair,
Strutting proudly down the street,
With every gaze a startled stare,
It's a joyfully clumsy treat.

Pineapple on pizza, what a debate,
Friends argue with playful cheer,
Yet in this clash, we celebrate,
Finding flavor in all we hold dear.

Each silly slip and each delight,
Threads of laughter weave so fast,
In quirky moments, joy takes flight,
And the silliness forever lasts.

The Art of Finding Joy in Chaos

Amongst the clutter and the spree,
A rubber duck floats on by,
In a sea of socks and lost keys,
Who knew chaos could soar high?

A blender hums a funky tune,
As smoothies swirl with glee,
In every sip, a hint of June,
A dance of wild energy.

When the dog steals a whole loaf,
And munches without a care,
We laugh together, building growth,
In moments that we share.

Every twist and every turn,
Brings a smile, a joyful face,
In the mess, we start to learn,
That chaos often finds its grace.

The Warmth of a Cuddle

In the chill of a winter night,
Two bodies twist and turn tight.
Laughter spills like hot cocoa,
A tug on a pillow, and off we go.

Blankets swaddle our giggles bright,
Frogs leap, and we squeal in delight.
Tickles transform into a ticklish race,
A cozy wrestle, what a fun place!

With snuggles that carry silly cheer,
We gleefully ask for just one more year.
Under moonlight, our secrets spill,
Wrapped up in warmth, we can't sit still.

A cuddle-filled journey that never ends,
One can never have too many friends.
With sly smiles and playful scuffles too,
In every snuggle, there's always something new.

Sunflower Smiles

Beneath the sky, where bright things grow,
A field of faces, all in a row.
Winking petals with sunny flair,
They sway in rhythm, dance without a care.

Chasing the shadow, they giggle and twist,
An unending party, how could we resist?
Whimsical whispers blow through their stalks,
As bees share tales and take cheerful walks.

A sunflower grins, its gaze on the sun,
With every tickle of breeze, it's all in fun.
When the harvest comes, it's a jolly affair,
In the kitchen, they cook up laughter to share.

So here's to blooms that cheerfully beam,
Each petal a wink, a playful dream.
In fields of glory, with color and cheer,
Sunflower smiles bring joy far and near.

The Dance of Chance Encounters

On bustling streets where stories collide,
A slip and a trip on a slippery slide.
Oops, I dropped my coffee cup,
And hats go flying, oh, what a mix-up!

With awkward apologies and shy little winks,
We find ourselves chuckling at life's funny kinks.
A nod, a grin, sparks fly between,
In the middle of chaos, we often glean.

Fates intertwine in the most silly ways,
Like dancing on ice during cold winter days.
Unplanned meetings, they're quirks in the plot,
What started as panic, now laughs that we've got.

So here's to the moments that take us off guard,
In laughter and joy, we're never too scarred.
For when the unexpected waltzes into view,
It's the spice of the story, bright and new!

The Magic of a Wink

A glance, a nudge, it all starts small,
With a wink, the world feels gall.
Unexpected giggles fill the air,
As secrets bloom, a playful affair.

Every blink a promise, a joke yet to share,
With fables and tales that dance everywhere.
A mystery beckons, hidden in a smile,
In the essence of magic, let's linger a while.

A wink can sway the dullest of days,
Turning gray skies into whimsical plays.
Among friends, it's a playful code,
What grand adventures down this road!

So flicker your eye, let laughter ignite,
In this realm of mischief, all feels so right.
For in every sparkle, a story awaits,
Let's chase them together, before it's too late.

Giggles in the Wind

Whispers dance on breezy trails,
A tickle sent through pants that flail.
Frogs croak jokes in the pond's reflection,
As squirrels plot their next distraction.

Umbrellas turn inside out, in glee,
As puddles splash with a laughing spree.
The sun sneezes, and the clouds all quake,
In this merry world, giggles awake.

Bright Threads of Existence

A spider weaves a web of cheer,
Each strand a laugh, each knot sincere.
Grass tickles toes in a playful jest,
While butterflies flutter, never at rest.

Colors burst like popcorn in a pan,
Laughter spills from every clan.
The sun seems bright, wearing glasses small,
And shadows sway like they're having a ball.

Flickers of Delight

A dance of fireflies in the dusk,
Their flickers bright, like confetti's husk.
Heat from the grill, burgers do tease,
While ants march on, under trees with ease.

A dog barks loud at nothing at all,
Chasing its tail, it begins to fall.
The moon laughs quietly at the scene,
As stars giggle at the night's routine.

The Weight of a Smile

A grin too broad will make you slip,
Like buttered toast or a wild road trip.
Gumdrops cheer from candy jars,
While cookies giggle beneath the stars.

Toasters pop with a toasted shout,
As morning spills what it's all about.
A dandelion whispers, 'Make a wish,'
In a world that's funny, just take a swish.

Secrets Beneath the Surface of Sunrise

A rooster struts, proud on his perch,
While thoughts of breakfast begin to lurch.
Eggs are cracking, laughter in the air,
As the sun stretches, without a care.

Muffins rise like cakes on a throne,
As shadows shift, all on their own.
Jokes from the toaster ready to burst,
In this morning scene, we quench our thirst.

Squirrels chatter, plotting the day,
They steal the nuts in a sneaky way.
The world awakes with playful delight,
As dawn tiptoes into the bright.

Whispers of warmth weave in the breeze,
Like secrets shared beneath the trees.
Amidst the giggles of sunbeams that sing,
Mornings bloom, funny as spring.

Giggles in the Garden of Time

In a garden where daisies wear crowns,
Marigolds chuckle, not a frown.
Bees buzzing tales of sweet delight,
They dance around, taking flight.

Rabbits hop with mischief in sight,
Chasing shadows in the soft twilight.
Flowers sway, gossiping away,
In this patch of green, they laugh and play.

Clouds drift by, dressed in plush white,
Playing hide and seek, oh what a sight!
A sunbeam tickles the grass below,
And laughter erupts from seeds that grow.

Moments like these are fleeting, it's true,
But in each smile, a memory grew.
In the garden, time trails its rhyme,
Here we find joy, even in grime.

Fleeting Glances and Frivolous Dreams

A wink from fate, with a giggle or two,
Fluttering leaves dance, a merry crew.
Chasing whims on a breeze that spins,
In this world of jest, where fun begins.

Clouds puff past, in playful arcs,
While crickets serenade with their sparks.
Dreams flit by like butterflies bright,
In a whimsical chase, pure delight.

Surprises peek from behind the tree,
Where whispers of glee playfully flee.
Frogs croak sonnets, oh so grand,
As smiles bloom across this land.

Time ticks gently, a soft, sly tease,
Yet in these moments, hearts find ease.
Fleeting shadows laugh and sway,
Crafting magic in a silly ballet.

The Playful Dance of Shadows and Light

Twilight giggles, colors collide,
As shadows twirl, they can't hide.
Moonlight winks, a cheeky display,
Filling the night with a grand array.

Stars peek out with a mischievous grin,
Inviting whispers of secrets within.
Footsteps echo in a playful chase,
While dreams spin quickly, setting the pace.

Branches sway to the rhythm of night,
Playing tag with beams soft and light.
Laughter drifts on the cool evening air,
As the world dons a whimsical flair.

In this ballet, sweet mischief exists,
Where every blink contains playful twists.
Shadows dance in their frolicsome spree,
Creating a tapestry, wild and free.

A Canvas of Memories

Painted skies and silly songs,
We dance around where time prolongs.
A splash of joy, a dash of cheer,
Each moment shared, our laughter near.

Colors blend like old friends do,
With every brush, a story new.
We scribble dreams in playful hues,
And smile at paths we've often choosed.

A canvas stretched, with splatters bright,
In shadows, we find hidden light.
With every stroke, a twist of fate,
Together we find what makes us great.

Frames of laughter, corners spun,
In the gallery, we have our fun.
Each memory a masterpiece bold,
In silly tales, our hearts unfold.

Stories in Every Breath

Whispers dance on the evening breeze,
   Tales of fish that joke with keys.
  Smiles are traded, secrets shared,
    In every sigh, adventure dared.

From wobbly steps to stumbly grace,
   We giggle at our awkward race.
  A yarn unraveled, a twist or two,
    In the melody, a quirky view.

In every chuckle, a story's spun,
With every breath, our hearts have fun.
As clouds drift by, our thoughts may roam,
  But silly tales will always be home.

With each heartbeat, the rhythm's sweet,
 In laughter's warmth, we find our seat.
 So take a breath, let the stories flow,
   In every pause, let joy be shown.

Happiness in a Teardrop

A teardrop rolls, a funny sight,
Like rainbows born from stormy night.
With giggles hiding, it softly falls,
Cracking up in the silence of halls.

Dancing down, it shares its tales,
Of clumsy slips and silly fails.
Moments fleeting, yet full of glee,
In puddles formed, we laugh with free.

In sadness wrapped, a silly grin,
For in the fumble, joy begins.
Wipe that tear, see laughter bright,
In every drop, a spark of light.

So bring your woes, lay down your cares,
We'll turn them into cheeky flares.
With every tear, a chuckle grows,
In the mess of life, laughter flows.

Glimmers of the Unexpected

Where shadows play and corners hide,
Surprises wait on the silly side.
A sudden giggle, a burst of cheer,
In moments paused, the winks appear.

The cat that zooms on flying feet,
Or shoes that squeak with every beat.
A wardrobe mishap, a slip, a trip,
With every crash, our spirits flip.

Out of the blue, a riddle's born,
A why that leaves us oh so torn.
With puzzled brows, we scratch and sigh,
Yet in that glance, we simply fly.

So raise a toast to the night's surprise,
To goofy looks and blinkered eyes.
In the twists and turns, we find our spark,
Through unexpected laughs that light the dark.

A Symphony of Grins

In the circus of our days, we play,
Juggling dreams like kids at play.
A wink, a smile, a wink in return,
Golden glories we all discern.

Balloons that float and squirrels that dance,
Wobbling on a tightrope of chance.
The clown's big shoes, so oversized,
Trip over laughter, not surprised.

With tickles and chuckles, we paint our fate,
A cake of joy we celebrate.
Every stumble becomes a jive,
Our silly hearts feel so alive.

In this orchestra of silly glee,
A symphony of smiles, come join me.
Together we'll dance on this wild spree,
With giggles and grins, we're always free.

Tiny Triumphs

A butterfly lands on a toe,
And suddenly, we're in the flow.
Every tiny win is a spark,
Like finding a treasure in the dark.

Dancing with shadows, we take a chance,
Clumsy, yet we still twirl and prance.
A paper plane soars high and wide,
In mini victories, we take great pride.

The cat that leaps but lands in a spin,
A comic tale, the laughter begins.
In little things, joy always thrives,
Tiny triumphs keep our spark alive.

Grab a snack, share a grin,
Every bite brings the cheer within.
With playful hearts and a cheer so bright,
We savor small wins, day and night.

Glimmers in the Gloom

Amid the clouds, a sunbeam peeks,
A cheeky grin that softly speaks.
When times are tough and shadows loom,
We find our way, dispelling gloom.

A duck in rain boots, splashing around,
Dancing puddles on the ground.
With silly hats and silly socks,
We laugh off woes, unlock the locks.

Glimmers sparkle in murky seas,
A spark of joy upon the breeze.
Through storms we soar, on laughter's wings,
In little jokes, sweet laughter sings.

As whispers of hope weave through the day,
We navigate our quirky way.
With every chuckle, we bloom and grow,
And find our light in the undertow.

Strokes of Brilliance

A paintbrush dipped in silly dreams,
We splash our canvas with goofy gleams.
Every stroke, a chirpy chime,
Artful moments we craft in rhyme.

Sprinkling colors on our fate,
With twirls and twirls, we celebrate.
A splash of red, a dash of blue,
Creating wonders in all we do.

The tickle of brush on canvas bright,
Grows a portrait in pure delight.
Through smears and splats, we make it shine,
In the mess of colors, we intertwine.

With whimsical strokes, we swirl around,
Art laughs at rules, breaks safe and sound.
In playful chaos, brilliance stirs,
Creating magic in our blurs.

Whispers of a Curious Heart

A cat in a hat danced on a wall,
Chasing its tail, it begins to sprawl.
An old man with shoes three sizes too small,
Sips tea with a mouse, oh what a ball!

Children with crayons draw skies that are green,
While ants in a line act like they're mean.
A cow in a tutu twirls with delight,
Under a disco ball shining so bright.

Fish play chess beneath the cool sea,
Arguing over who's as clever as me.
A bird on a swing sings songs from the past,
Time stretches and bends, nothing's ever fast.

Lemonade rivers flow through the park,
Where shadows of giggles create their mark.
With each silly step, the heart begins to leap,
In a world where secrets dance, oh so deep.

Echoes of Everyday Smiles

A dust bunny whispers from under the couch,
Sometimes it giggles, sometimes it slouch.
A toaster pops toast like fireworks in spring,
Each slice of bread a salute it can bring.

Rabbits in bowties hop over the hills,
While mushrooms play tag among daffodil thrills.
A squirrel in a vest is selling free hugs,
Trading them gently for warm coffee mugs.

The clock chimes a tune that's less about time,
Instead it hums sweetly, like poetry's rhyme.
Umbrellas parade in the sunshine so bold,
Sharing their secrets of adventures untold.

At twilight, the stars play a game of charades,
While shadows of laughter in the evening cascade.
A picnic of giggles, snacks piled high,
Under the watch of a twinkling sky.

The Joys Hidden in Mundane Moments

Tea bags are wizards, steeping in wait,
Turning hot water to magic on a plate.
As spoons do the cha-cha in the kitchen drawer,
Pots and pans join in, asking for more.

The simple act of walking to the store,
Becomes a grand journey, an explorer's lore.
Tossed in the wind, leaves swirl and boast,
Each with a story, a seasonal toast.

Paperclips fight like gladiators in lines,
While candy wrappers giggle, sharing their wines.
A sock with a hole dreams of playing the flute,
And a stubborn old chair has a crush on a boot.

When shadows stretch long in the fading light,
It's not just the end, but the start of the night.
In the quilt of our days, the threads weave so fine,
With patches of laughter, we find our own shine.

Tiny Wonders in a Great Big World

A snail on a mission, with a suitcase in tow,
Travels the garden, taking it slow.
Each raindrop's a pebble, a marvel in fall,
As puddles become oceans, so vast and so tall.

A leaf on the breeze does cartwheels of gold,
While dreams of the sun come gently unfold.
A dog with a crown claims the park as its throne,
Barking orders at ducks, in a regal tone.

Bubbles from soap taste like laughter and cheer,
Floating away with no worries or fear.
Each giggle's a treasure, a glint in the sun,
Reminding us all how to frolic and run.

The universe whispers in colors so bright,
While shadows do ballet in the warm autumn light.
In the small, tender moments we often ignore,
Lies magic that dances forever and more.

The Color of a Giggle

A splash of bright, a sprinkle of cheer,
Chasing shadows, wiping a tear.
Laughter twirls on a summer breeze,
Painting each moment with playful ease.

Tickles of joy in the air we breathe,
Woven tales that we never leave.
With every chuckle, the world seems fine,
The color of happiness, a sweet sunshine.

When jokes collide, like stars in the night,
We dance with the stars, oh what a sight!
Each smile a brush, each wink a hue,
In the gallery of life, I'd frame me and you.

So gather those giggles, let them reside,
In corners of hearts where secrets hide.
For every chuckle holds magic in store,
A canvas of joy, forever to explore.

Notes of a Gentle Heart

Music in whispers, soft as a sigh,
Tickles of rhythm that flutter and fly.
Every note carries a tale to unfold,
In the quietest moments, wonders behold.

Strumming on dreams, a banjo's sweet call,
Gentle reminders, we're part of it all.
With each gentle pulse, the universe spins,
Finding comfort in chaos, that's where it begins.

Chirps of the dawn, in symphonic delight,
Breezy refrains in the soft morning light.
With laughter as lyrics, we sing our way through,
A ballad of kindness, forever anew.

So play on your heartstrings, and let them ring true,
In the concert of living, I'll dance close to you.
For notes of affection are sweet melodies,
A gentle reminder of love's soft breeze.

Vignettes of Joyous Existence

Snapshots of smiles, moments that beam,
Time's fleeting treasure, like wisps of a dream.
Each giggle a glimpse, a slip of delight,
A tangle of stories that dance in the light.

Photographs hanging on memory's wall,
Colors of humor that never grow small.
Twirling through laughter, we trace with our feet,
In vignettes of joy, the world feels complete.

With hats made of sunshine and shoes full of cheer,
We skip through the puddles, embrace every year.
Every misstep a masterpiece drawn,
In this art of existence, we laugh at the dawn.

So treasure the moments, the fleeting, the fun,
In this kaleidoscope life, we're forever young.
For each joyous nibble and whimsical glance,
Is a snapshot of laughter, a glorious dance.

Sunbeams and Daydreams

Waking to sunshine, a warm, gentle kiss,
Frolicking clouds, oh, don't we feel bliss?
With thoughts that drift on a breeze full of play,
In the soft embrace of a lighthearted day.

Picnic blankets sprawled on the grass so green,
Every bite savored, laughter between.
As daisies chat with the bees in delight,
We're stitching the moments, so snug and so bright.

Chasing the shadows, we leap and we twirl,
In the frolic of time, watch the joy unfurl.
Each smile is a sunbeam, brightening the way,
In a collage of dreams that won't fade away.

So dance with the sunlight, and dream with the stars,
In this silly old world, we can't help but spar.
For every bright ray offers magic and schemes,
Together we soar, on sunbeams and daydreams.

Chasing Shadows

In the park, they run around,
Juggling dreams that hit the ground.
Chasing ducks and paper planes,
Laughter echoing like silly trains.

Do you see that dancing tree?
It whispers tales of what could be.
A shadow prancing, quite absurd,
Making faces, like a bird!

With every twist and playful spin,
They chase the joy that's deep within.
Silly giggles, full of glee,
The heart sings bright, wild, and free.

And when the sun begins to set,
They'll catch the night, no time to fret.
For in each moment, bright and bold,
A treasure in the laughter told.

The Dance of Everyday

Waking up to socks that fight,
Coffee brews with morning light.
Toasters pop like little drums,
While breakfast dances, here it comes!

In the office, chairs do glide,
As coworkers gently slide.
Notes and doodles on the side,
A silent vote for joy, no pride.

Lunch breaks bring a food ballet,
Sandwiches pirouette and sway.
Chasing crumbs that roll away,
As laughter takes the lead in play.

The clock ticks on, the day unfolds,
In every laugh, a tale retold.
In this dance, straightforward yet bright,
Every step's a sheer delight.

Marvels in the Mundane

A dusty car that dreams of speed,
Waves at clouds and takes the lead.
Raindrops, like a drummer's beat,
Tap-dancing on the sidewalk's seat.

In every corner, wonders wait,
Lost socks mock the hands of fate.
A cat that snores, a dog that sings,
As everyday's a dance of wings.

The grocery line, a show in queue,
With squabbling carts that loudly woo.
Bananas toss in playful cheer,
A woman's laugh is loud and clear.

So here we find the great unknown,
In simple moments brightly shown.
Each little giggle, a sparkling chance,
To see the world in a silly dance.

Revelations Under Starlight

Beneath the stars, the whispers start,
A picnic blanket close at heart.
The moon provides a silver stage,
For fireflies to dance and engage.

In hidden dreams, the shadows giggle,
As night reveals a secret wiggle.
What if clouds wore silly hats?
And trees could tell jokes with sassy spats?

A shooting star, a fleeting grin,
On pathways where the fun begins.
Count the wishes, lose the frowns,
As laughter splashes like raindrops' crowns.

So gather round and share your tales,
For in the night, our laughter sails.
In shared delights beneath the haze,
We find the spark in starry gaze.

Paths of Wonder

Each twist and turn brings a grin,
A squirrel's dance, a cheeky spin.
With every step, quirks take flight,
A world of giggles, pure delight.

Beneath the trees, the shadows play,
Tickling toes in a silly way.
The clouds conspire, shapes they weave,
Chasing dreams on a bright reprieve.

We stumble forth, paths we create,
Chasing shadows, tempting fate.
With laughter echoing in the air,
Adventures bloom, beyond compare.

In the end, it's clear to see,
The wilder, the better, we must agree!
With every laugh, a moment won,
A path of wonder under the sun.

Sips of Serenity

In a cup, a tiny storm,
A sprinkle of joy, a cheerful norm.
Swirls of cream, a sweet parade,
With each sip, worries fade.

A giggle erupts from the brew,
Who knew the kettle had a view?
Tea leaves whisper their secrets old,
Tales of warmth, adventures bold.

Sugar cubes dance, a flair so grand,
Marshmallows float like clouds on sand.
Every gulp, a chuckle shared,
In this moment, we are ensnared.

With each sip, serenity flows,
A world of whimsy, how it glows.
So raise your cup to the joyful blend,
In this simple brew, we transcend.

Threads of Happiness

In a loom of colors bright,
Tiny threads weave pure delight.
Every stitch, a chuckle sewn,
Crafting joy, never alone.

A patchwork quilt of silly dreams,
With quirky patterns, or so it seems.
Each square a tale, a joke, a jest,
In the cozy folds, we find our rest.

Laughter threads through every seam,
Fluffy clouds and ice cream dreams.
We tug and pull, create a tune,
In this fabric, we find a boon.

From tangled knots to spinning bliss,
The warmth of friendship, a sweet kiss.
Together we stitch this radiant bend,
In a tapestry where giggles blend.

A Tapestry of Whimsy

Woven paths in a world so bright,
Dancing daisies in the sunlight.
Stray balloons with faces wide,
A parade of silliness on the ride.

Colors burst in playful hues,
A jigsaw puzzle with giggly clues.
Butterflies wear hats so grand,
In this realm, we all can stand.

Riddles float on a gentle breeze,
When tickled by the swaying trees.
Every corner holds a spark,
A wild balloon dog in the park.

With every twist of fate we find,
A quirky moment left behind.
In this tapestry where fun resides,
A playful heart forever abides.

Playful Shadows

In the garden, shadows play,
Twisting figures dance away.
A cat pretends to be a ghost,
Chasing sunlight, it loves the most.

Under trees, the giggles float,
A squirrel stirs, steals a coat.
They schemed, plotted from the top,
While I sat and couldn't stop.

Bright ideas fly and flare,
But it's just a lost old hare.
With every wink the sun won't cry,
Oh, how time just loves to fly!

The whispers spin from dusk till dawn,
Confusion reigns, the cards are drawn.
As shadows waltz, we stomp our feet,
In this circus, can't be beat!

Mischief in the Breeze

A breeze blows in, oh what a tease,
Tugging hats and flapping leaves.
Buttons pop and shoelaces fly,
As giggles chase the clouds up high.

Kites are tangled, oh what a sight,
A dog runs mad in sheer delight.
A balloon floats, oh where's it off?
Waving goodbye, answers scoff.

Bumblebees buzz through flower beds,
Tickling toes and bouncing heads.
A bee on a mission, nectar in tow,
While we chase, it steals the show!

So we dance in this jolly mess,
With mismatched socks, we feel the stress.
But laughter rolls in tides of spree,
In this whimsical cacophony!

Serene Explorations

In quiet nooks where wonders bloom,
I spy a frog, singing its tune.
Pondering why the sun gets shy,
As stars emerge to wink and sigh.

A turtle hugs its shell with flair,
While squirrels argue over a pear.
Each thought is granted, none dismissed,
As nature laughs at what we've missed.

A gentle stream hums tales of yore,
With whispers from the forest floor.
It tells of secrets, soft and near,
And my heart swells, oh dear, oh dear!

As moonlight drapes the waking world,
A tapestry of dreams unfurled.
We wander on this winding path,
With every step, we find the laugh.

Chasing Fireflies

In twilight's glow, the flickers spark,
Tiny lights dance in the dark.
We race with glee, arms open wide,
In this game where giggles abide.

Little lanterns, bright and bold,
Whisper secrets yet untold.
They twirl about, just out of reach,
While we plot and plan to teach.

Patience falters, the chase is on,
As shadows stretch and the daylight's gone.
With jars in hand, we catch but few,
Yet oh, the joy in moments anew!

So here's to nights of flying dreams,
Where fun is found in fleeting beams.
Each spark a promise, each laugh a thread,
In the tapestry of all we've said!

Gentle Echoes

In the quiet of a chuckle, so light,
A cat on a skateboard gives quite a fright.
With a leap and a bound, the dog takes his cue,
As they whizz past the sun, what a comical view.

When toast lands butter-side down on the floor,
The universe giggles, can't help but roar.
A sock in the dryer begins to conspire,
While the other socks plot to escape and retire.

With every small stumble, a giggle we find,
A dance of the clumsy, so joyful, combined.
A sneeze turns to laughter, a fit of surprise,
In the mirror's reflection, a joke in disguise.

So gather your chuckles, let's brighten the day,
In a waltz of the goofy, we twirl and we sway.
With echoes so gentle, and joy in the air,
We find all the humor in moments we share.

A Dash of the Unexpected

In the kitchen, a blender takes flight with a roar,
As oranges circle, a citrus galore.
Pancakes flip high, with a burst and a splat,
Who knew breakfast could look quite like that?

A bird on a leash thinks it's taking a stroll,
While a squirrel in a hoodie dreams big, oh so bold.
At the park, a kid tries to juggle some pies,
With whipped cream disasters, laughter fills the skies.

An umbrella that flips on a windy quick dance,
Turns a rainy day into a comical chance.
With puddles that splash and boots running wild,
Even grumpy faces become brightly styled.

So cherish the quirks, the twists in the plot,
For every surprise is a giggle you've caught.
With a dash of the funny, we sway and we glide,
In moments so silly, our hearts open wide.

Sunsets and Silly Stories

When the sun starts to bow with a wink and a grin,
Cats gather round for a mischievous spin.
A dog in a cape pounces over the hill,
While shadows play tag, and the night starts to chill.

A fairytale spider spins webs with a glee,
And leaves us all guessing what might it be.
The breeze whispers secrets, like tickles of air,
On the edges of twilight, we laugh without care.

The moon clears its throat with a chuckle so bright,
As stars start their giggles, lighting up the night.
With stories of wonders and mischief galore,
We gather together, always wanting more.

So let the tales linger, like echoes of fun,
As sunsets paint laughter, until day is done.
In a world full of quirks, we dance and we roam,
With every silly story, we craft our own home.

Vows of the Heart

With a wink and a nudge, we promise to play,
Through rain or through sunshine, come what may.
A wink followed by giggles, hand in hand we stand,
In a circus of laughter, our dreams understand.

The vows we create, they twist and they twirl,
Like a pancake that flops, oh what a swirl!
In the chaos of warmth, we find a sweet tune,
With mischief as timeless as stars and the moon.

We'll dance through the kitchen, the socks on the floor,
With love mixed with humor, who could ask for more?
When calamity strikes, we'll both catch a grin,
As we navigate life, it's the joy where we win.

So here's to our journey, with giggles anew,
In the vows of our hearts, we'll write our own view.
In a world filled with whimsy, we proudly declare,
To laugh and to love, in adventures we share.

Notes from a Kindred Spirit

Whispers of joy fill the air,
With giggles of gnomes everywhere.
A dance with the socks, oh what a sight,
As they twirl in the sunlight, shining bright.

Chasing butterflies in a shoe,
Wearing hats made of soup, who knew?
Tickles from the breeze, softly played,
In a world where fun is always displayed.

Bananas slip, a comic show,
Toasters pop sparks, oh what a glow!
Cats in ties reading the news,
Sharing secrets wrapped in the blues.

Colors bounce off the page,
Like sprightly kids in a playful rage.
Each chuckle is a spark, a ray,
In realms of mirth where we can stay.

Petals of Laughter

A sunflower grins at the curious bee,
Telling tales of sweet jubilee.
While worms in bowties wiggle with glee,
Under the shade of the giggling tree.

Clouds gather round with a playful cheer,
Making faces that bring us near.
Raindrops dance with a jolly jig,
Splashes so bright, as large as a pig.

Socks on dogs race in the yard,
Each one thinking they try too hard.
Silly hats and shoes abound,
As joy skips and hops all around.

Petals twirl with the tickling breeze,
Unveiling secrets of happy keys.
A chorus of chuckles fills the day,
In this whimsical, sunny array.

Wandering Thoughts

A duck in a tux, swaying on the pond,
Sharing secrets with a deer, so fond.
The stars giggle down from way up high,
While dreamers ponder why clouds pass by.

Cacti wear sunglasses, feeling so cool,
Whispers of joy, their golden rule.
Rabbits with shoes dance through the grass,
In a world where time surely won't pass.

Jellybeans jump with a bounce and flare,
While gumdrops giggle in candy air.
Each moment a jest, each hour a jest,
In the garden where humor is best dressed.

Wandering thoughts on a bright blue day,
Like butterflies lost in a breezy ballet.
A chuckle or two, a smile wide,
Through the avenues where joy doth reside.

Gems of Glee

A pebble in puddles makes ripples of fun,
While dimples of sunshine dance with the sun.
Pancakes flip high in a buttery twirl,
As giggles of syrup begin to swirl.

Kites in the sky, like dreams on a rope,
Float high with the breeze, filled with hope.
A parrot sings jokes as it struts on the line,
Spreading more chuckles, so sweet and divine.

Zebras in pajamas prance through the night,
Counting the stars till the morning light.
Turtles in hats and fish with a grin,
Reveal the secrets of joy from within.

Gems of glee in this quirky spree,
Sparkling bright, oh can't you see?
Let laughter ring out, from every soul,
In the treasure chest where humor is whole.

Tiny Revelations

The cat on the roof turned a bright shade of blue,
Chasing shadows from dusk until the dawn broke through.

A squirrel wore sunglasses, all stylish and neat,
As it danced with the wind, no worries or defeat.

The clock ticked slowly, or so it did seem,
Every second a chance for a whimsical dream.
With a wink and a giggle, the flowers would sway,
As they whispered their secrets in a comical way.

A dog with a hat thought it ruled the whole block,
While the trees played the game of a well-timed knock.
The puddles reflected the skies full of cheer,
As they laughed at the clouds for their silly veneer.

With ice cream patience, we search for the clue,
In the nonsense of choices, so vibrant and true.
The ducks in a row march, though not very straight,
Finding humor in everything, never too late.

Echoes of Laughter

A frog in a tuxedo hops onto the scene,
Singing songs of the pond like a regal machine.
With each leap he insists, "It's a dance you should try!"
While the lilies applaud with a warm, gentle sigh.

A penguin at brunch sips his tea with a twist,
With secrets in scones that just can't be missed.
He tells tales of snowflakes with a wink and a grin,
While the toast pops up, capturing mischief within.

The mirrors all giggle, reflecting the fun,
As they twist and they turn under rays of the sun.
A banana slips past with a comic parade,
While humor is sewn in each silly charade.

The bubble of laughter floats up to the sky,
Tickling stars as they giggle and sigh.
In the heart of the moment, we find pure delight,
With echoes of joy that stretch through the night.

Fleeting Joys

A kite in the wind, oh, what a grand sight,
It zooms and it dances, taking off in flight.
With colors so vivid, it paints the blue skies,
While children below wear surprise in their eyes.

A clown on a bike, balancing high,
Juggling away as the birds dash by.
With each little giggle, he winks at the crowd,
And the daisies all cheer, feeling light and proud.

An orange slice giggles, perched on a plate,
As it whispers to lemons, "We're feeling just great!"
With laughter that flutters, like butterflies do,
Turning moments to magic, in colors so true.

As raindrops cascade, a tap dance begins,
To the rhythms of puddles, where nonsense wins.
With twinkling conversations wrapped up in a bow,
Fleeting joys surround us, in warm afterglow.

Secrets in the Leaves

The leaves tell a story in rustles and sways,
Of journeys and giggles in sunlit arrays.
A squirrel's tiny party with acorns to share,
In a festive debate of who's got the best hair!

A flutter of fairies marked yesterday's trend,
As they danced through the branches, with laughter to lend.
With a sprinkle of magic, they painted the air,
While the trees rolled their eyes at a leaky repair.

A whispering wind carries tales quite profound,
Of friendships unbroken, spun round and round.
The petals all chuckle, in the warm summer breeze,
As they twirl and they sway, sharing secrets with ease.

Beneath all the chatter, sweet giggles and sighs,
Linger softly, as wisdom in nature complies.
So let's gather our laughter, like leaves in a heap,
And toss them in air, for the joy we will keep.

The Unexpected Brightness

A penguin tried to ride a bike,
It wobbled, and oh, what a sight!
With one flipper up, it took a chance,
Spinning circles like a clumsy dance.

A turtle wore a straw hat,
Claiming it's a high-class brat.
Strutting slow, he'd flip a shell,
Saying, "Fast is overrated, can't you tell?"

A cat that whispers to the moon,
Asks, "Dear friend, will we spoon?"
The night just blinks and twirls away,
Leaving the cat to dream and play.

A duck debates the stars above,
Saying, "They aren't what I dream of!"
Quacking loud, with a twist of fate,
"Fish are funny, but I'd rather skate!"

Embracing the Quirk

A goat in glasses reads the news,
While sipping tea from shiny blues.
He laughs at headlines, gives a grin,
Says, "Why on earth are we so thin?"

The socks in drawers begin to fight,
A polka dot vs. stripes so bright.
They argue loudly, make a scene,
'Til freed, they dance like none have seen.

A fish who thinks it's real profound,
Wiggles tales of the sea, renowned.
With bubbles forming, it takes a stand,
"Who needs feet? I'm in command!"

A chair that dreams of flying high,
Wants to join the clouds and sky.
It squeaks and creaks, a hopeful plea,
"Just let me go, I'll be so free!"

Little Sparks of Delight

A sneeze turns into a spark,
A laugh echoes in the park.
Life's oddities, a curious blend,
In hiccups of joy, we transcend.

A penguin slips, a banana peel,
The joke's on us, what a surreal feel!
With winks and nods, the world spins round,
In giggles and grins, true joy is found.

Frogs in tuxedos play a show,
While flowers discuss the weather, you know!
Each step a dance, each thought a turn,
In this delightful circus, we learn.

So let hearts flutter like butterflies,
Chasing starlight in the skies.
With every twist that fate imparts,
We find the warmth in silly hearts.

The Enigma of Grins and Whims

A cat wears glasses, reading a tome,
With a twitchy tail, it stirs in its dome.
In shadows, secrets softly creep,
Whispers of magic, dreams to keep.

Where socks go missing, adventures begin,
A quality met in where we've been.
With spools of yarn and paper planes,
We unravel mysteries and silly gains.

The moon grins wide, a pie in the sky,
While bats hold meetings with butterflies.
Each chuckle a riddle, each snicker a clue,
Painting our stories in vibrant hue.

Through mirror mazes, we march unrestricted,
With every twist, laughter's scripted.
In this riddle of whimsy, we're bound to roam,
Finding magic in the absurd we call home.

Delicate Riddles of the Ordinary

A teacup dances on the edge,
Making bets with the kettle's pledge.
A toast to hiccups, a nod to cheese,
In simple moments, we find our ease.

The puzzle of toast, that lands buttered side down,
Turns everyday frowns into a crown.
With mismatched socks and a quirky grin,
Every mundane task leads to a win.

Birds debate the angle of flight,
As insects plot the party tonight.
In a jumble of thoughts, we find our path,
With silken threads of playful math.

So gather the giggles and dance with delight,
In lurking shadows, the ordinary's bright.
Amongst the riddles, joy's never far,
As we twirl through our world, a shining star.

Mischief in the Margins of Existence

A squirrel in shades sips lemonade,
Plotting a heist in the summer parade.
With a wink and a wiggle, oh what a tease,
The mischief they brew floats like a breeze.

The grass whispers secrets to wandering toes,
While clouds play tag as the sun bestows.
In the quiet chaos, a giggle erupts,
From sprightly critters, their antics corrupt.

Each moment a caper, each day a trick,
With shadows that dance and voices that flick.
In the margins of scuffles and playful glee,
We find ourselves grinning, wild and free.

So tiptoe through laughter, let whimsy preside,
In this merry suspense, let folly abide.
As joy's little misfits leap into sight,
We're caught in a whirlwind, ever so light.

www.ingramcontent.com/pod-product-compliance
Lightning Source LLC
Chambersburg PA
CBHW051650160426
43209CB00004B/857